AF823442

The Brilliant Content Planner

Barbara Grassey

Copyright 2017. Barbara Grassey.

All Rights Reserved. No portion of this book may be reproduced, stored in a retrieval system, or transcribed in any form or by any means—electronic, mechanical, photocopy, recording, scanning, or other without the prior written consent of the author/publisher.

ISBN: 978-0998394701

Table of Contents

Hi,

I'm Barbara Grassey, the Book Boss.

I've been writing since I was a little kid, but just over ten years ago I stepped into my dreams and started writing for a living. And you know what?

It's a lot of work! (But I LOVE IT!)

Here's what I've learned:

If you're going to be in business today, you need to put out VALUABLE CONTENT – things your potential clients and current clients need to know. But staying organized and on schedule can be a full time job.

I finally developed worksheets that allowed me to organize myself, my blog, and my podcast. Now I KNOW what I am going to be writing about. I can do all the research for a month's worth of posts in one batch and most importantly, I can give my readers and listeners a well thought out path of knowledge.

And now I'm sharing my content organizing secrets with you!

LET'S GET GOING!

Your Brilliant Content Planner includes:

- Brainstorming Prompts
- Brain Dump Worksheet
- Keyword Worksheet
- Yearly Content Arc
- Monthly Topic Sheet
- Monthly Tracking and Sharing Charts
- Content Worksheets

Let's Connect!

Facebook.com/BarbaraGrasseyBookCoach

Twitter.com/BarbBookBoss

LinkedIn.com/in/BarbaraGrassey

Barbara@BarbaraGrassey.com

How to Use this Planner

Note: If you have purchased the "printable" version of this Planner, save this file, then print out the pages. You can also save the file, make changes to the worksheets to customize them for your needs, and then resave the file under a different name. This way you can keep the original file "clean" to reuse for years to come.

The first section of the planner (before the worksheets) helps you decide on your overall content for the year. (And, your year can start at any point.)

Whether you are using this for your blog, podcast, or to plan out your YouTube videos, start with answering the **Brainstorming Prompts**. Then do the "**Brain Dump**." Just jot down any ideas you may have. There's no particular order and at this point, no idea is bad or dumb. You're just getting all those ideas out of your head and onto paper so you don't have to worry about forgetting something brilliant. Keep the list handy—you can add over the course of a week or the year.

One of the best ways to plan your content, is to take your audience on a transformational journey. The **Yearly Content Arc** is designed to help you plan out a logical progression for your readers. Ideally, you want that progression to lead people to what you are offering at various points along the way. Working with an overall plan helps you to ensure that you don't forget to make your offers!

The **Monthly Topic List** helps create a coherent flow to your posts and podcasts. You can have a monthly "theme" where you talk about one aspect of your niche and have each post build on the last. You might also want to set up posts where once a month you do a special recurring post, such as a Tips and Tricks, New Tools, Interview, or Product Review.

I've also included a **Comprehensive Keyword List**. Knowing what terms people search on to find the information and services that you offer is invaluable to you. You want your posts to be keyword rich, which is why I recommend using an SEO plugin such as SEO Yoast, on your blog and using keywords in your podcast and video descriptions. Having a pre-made list (one that you can add to, of course!) will make it easier to ensure that you are taking full advantage of organic search.

Your Initial Metrics and **Monthly Metrics Tracking Sheets**: You need to know where you are starting from in order to see if your new content plan is doing its job. The Initial Metrics sheet marks your starting point. If you do not know how many people are visiting your individual blog post pages or downloading podcasts, those numbers are easy enough to find out. YouTube tracks number of views for you. Your podcast hosting company compiles your statistics—you may need to upgrade your hosting plan, but it is worth it to get those numbers. You can use Google Analytics on your site, or use the statistics programs that come bundled with your hosting company. Google Analytics provides more detailed numbers, but tracking in any form is a positive move.

Once you have written in your initial numbers, use the Monthly Metric Tracking Sheets to log in what is happening with your posts. You may find that you get more reaction to a certain type of post or more shares of another type. Make a note of all this so you can give your people more of what they want.

Here's the thing: When you first get started with metrics, it's kind of hard to figure them all out. So if you can only easily get the numbers for certain things, like the number of people on your email list or your Facebook and Twitter followers, start with those. As you get more comfortable, add in things like how many people hit each individual blog post or how many podcast downloads you had. Metrics are something you can build on—you don't have to do them all from the get-go.

Using the Share Tracker

In order to gain the most traction possible, you need to share your content a minimum of 12 times. We tend to put up a blog post, maybe send it out to our list, and put a link on a couple of social media sites.

It's time to get much more strategic. After all, you're putting in a lot of work to craft informative and helpful posts. You want to make sure as many people as possible see them!

If you don't have 12 places to share your posts, there's nothing wrong with (and you really SHOULD) sharing the post more than once on social media sites

The second part of Your Brilliant Content Planner consists of the **Monthly Content Overview** worksheets and **Post Planning Sheets**.

The Monthly Content Overview allows you to choose a topic or "theme" for the month and then decide on your post topics. You can also make note of any holidays or events that you might want to use in your posts. Your Monthly Goal might be adding a certain number of followers to your blog or converting a certain number of readers into clients. It may be to have people share your content. Setting out your goal for the month helps shape the content (including the calls to action) that you will create.

The Post Planning Sheets help you stay on track. List the 4-6 main ideas that you want to cover in the post or podcast. (These could become subheads if you like.) You can rearrange the order once you have the ideas down and you start writing. You want to make sure you have links, both to sources outside your site and to content within your site. The internal links help your bounce rate – people stay on your site longer and that helps you in the organic searches. (A site where people land for 10 seconds and bounce right off does not rank as highly as a site where people stay, navigate to several pages, and spend more time.) I highly recommend using SEO Yoast or a similar plugin for your blog – it's a built-in reminder to SEO your posts. I also use a "Click to Tweet" plugin and I am adding "content upgrades" to my blog posts – a little note to "click here" to optin for additional information that pertains to the post.

Have ideas to make this planner better? Let me know! Send an email to Barbara@BarbaraGrassey.com

Brain Storming Prompts

Start by listing out areas within your niche that you want to talk about on your blog:

___

___

___

What are the three most frequently asked questions from your prospects?

___

___

___

What are the three most common problems you solve for your clients?

___

___

___

What are some of the cool apps, websites, programs, etc. that you can share with people?

___

___

___

What are some myths about your niche that people need to be educated on?

___

___

___

What questions do you receive repeatedly from people that make you roll your eyes or shake your head?

____

____

____

Who are some people who have had success (your clients or just famous people) by following your program or a similar program?

____

____

____

What were some of your early mistakes? What did you learn from them? What would you do differently?

____

____

____

Is there something happening in the news right now that you can tie in or relate to your business?

____

____

____

Brain Dump

Yearly Content Arc

Where are your people now? ____

____

What do they want or think they need? ____________________________________

____

What do they actually need? ____

____

Where do they want to end up? What transformation are they seeking?

____

____

Monthly Topic List

Month 1: ____

Month 2: ____

Month 3: ____

Month 4: ____

Month 5: ____

Month 6: ____

Month 7: ____

Month 8: ____

Month 9: ____

Month 10: ____

Month 11: ____

Month 12: ____

FROM BLOG TO BOOK

Do you know what a year of content is? A BOOK! Learn how you can re-purpose your blog content into a book that you can use as a lead generator or just an additional income stream.

When you're ready, go to BarbaraGrassey.com/from-blog-to-book

Comprehensive Keyword List

Long Tail or Keyword Phrases

Your Initial Metrics

That which is measured improves.

-- Karl Pearson

Starting Date: ______________________________

Metrics Last 3 Blog Posts/Podcasts/Videos

Date of Post: _______________ # of Visits: _______________

# of Comments _______________ # of Shares: _______________

Date of Post: _______________ # of Visits: _______________

# of Comments _______________ # of Shares: _______________

Date of Post: _______________ # of Visits: _______________

# of Comments _______________ # of Shares: _______________

Number of Subscribers on Mailing List: _______________

Number of Blog/Podcast/Channel Subscribers: _______________

Social Media Followers:

Facebook Business: _______________ Facebook Personal: _______________

LinkedIn: _______________ Twitter: _______________

Pinterest: _______________ Instagram: _______________

Other Social Media: _______________ Other Social Media: _______________

Average Product/Service Sales:

Product 1: _______________ Product 2: _______________

CONTENT WORKSHEETS

Monthly Content Overview

Month: ______________________________

Theme: ______________________________

Goal: ______________________________

Post 1 Title/Topic: ______________________________

Post 2 Title/Topic: ______________________________

Post 3 Title/Topic: ______________________________

Post 4 Title/Topic: ______________________________

Post 5 Title/Topic: ______________________________

Post 6 Title/Topic: ______________________________

Special This Month

Events/Holidays:

Any special promotions (product/service):

Monthly Metrics

		Post 1	Post 2	Post 3	Post 4	Post 5	Post 6	Other
# of Page Visits								
# New Subscribers (Added to List)								
# of Sales (if applicable)								
New Followers: Facebook								
New Followers: LinkedIn								
New Followers: Twitter								
New Followers: Pinterest								
New Followers: Instagram								
New Followers:								
New Followers:								
# of Comments on Blog								

Share Tracker

	Post 1	Post 2	Post 3	Post 4	Post 5	Post 6	Other	Special
Email/Subscriber List								
Facebook Personal Page								
Facebook Fan/Biz Page								
LinkedIn								
Twitter								
Instagram								
Pinterest								
Other Social Media								
Other Social Media								
Group or Forum								
Group or Forum								
YouTube								
Other								
Other								
Other								

Post 1 Title: ______________________________

Main Points:

____

____

____

____

____

____

Call to Action: ______________________________

Publication Date: ______________________________

Internal Links (Within Site):

____

____

External Links (Out of Site):

____

____

Click to Tweet: ________ Content Upgrade: ________

Images:

____

____

Post 2 Title: ____

Main Points:

____

____

____

____

____

____

Call to Action: ______________________________________

Publication Date: ____________________________________

Internal Links (Within Site):

____

____

External Links (Out of Site):

____

____

Click to Tweet: ________ Content Upgrade: ________

Images:

____

____

Post 3 Title: ______________________________

Main Points:

____

____

____

____

____

____

Call to Action: ______________________________

Publication Date: ______________________________

Internal Links (Within Site):

____

____

External Links (Out of Site):

____

____

Click to Tweet: ________ Content Upgrade: ________

Images:

____

____

Post 4 Title: ______________________________

Main Points:

____

____

____

____

____

____

Call to Action: ______________________________

Publication Date: ______________________________

Internal Links (Within Site):

____

____

External Links (Out of Site):

____

____

Click to Tweet: ________ Content Upgrade: ________

Images:

____

____

Post 5 Title: ______________________________

Main Points:

____

____

____

____

____

____

Call to Action: ______________________________

Publication Date: ______________________________

Internal Links (Within Site):

____

____

External Links (Out of Site):

____

____

Click to Tweet: ________ Content Upgrade: ________

Images:

____

____

Monthly Content Overview

Month: ______________________________

Theme: ______________________________

Goal: ______________________________

Post 1 Title/Topic: ______________________________

Post 2 Title/Topic: ______________________________

Post 3 Title/Topic: ______________________________

Post 4 Title/Topic: ______________________________

Post 5 Title/Topic: ______________________________

Post 6 Title/Topic: ______________________________

Special This Month

Events/Holidays:

Any special promotions (product/service):

Monthly Metrics

		Post 1	Post 2	Post 3	Post 4	Post 5	Post 6	Other
# of Page Visits								
# New Subscribers (Added to List)								
# of Sales (if applicable)								
New Followers: Facebook								
New Followers: LinkedIn								
New Followers: Twitter								
New Followers: Pinterest								
New Followers: Instagram								
New Followers:								
New Followers:								
# of Comments on Blog								

Share Tracker

	Post 1	Post 2	Post 3	Post 4	Post 5	Post 6	Other	Special
Email/Subscriber List								
Facebook Personal Page								
Facebook Fan/Biz Page								
LinkedIn								
Twitter								
Instagram								
Pinterest								
Other Social Media								
Other Social Media								
Group or Forum								
Group or Forum								
YouTube								
Other								
Other								
Other								

Post 1 Title: ______________________________

Main Points:

____

____

____

____

____

____

Call to Action: ______________________________

Publication Date: ______________________________

Internal Links (Within Site):

____

____

External Links (Out of Site):

____

____

Click to Tweet: ________ Content Upgrade: ________

Images:

____

____

Post 2 Title: ______________________________

Main Points:

____

____

____

____

____

____

Call to Action: ______________________________

Publication Date: ______________________________

Internal Links (Within Site):

____

____

External Links (Out of Site):

____

____

Click to Tweet: ________ Content Upgrade: ________

Images:

____

____

Post 3 Title: ____

Main Points:

____

____

____

____

____

____

Call to Action: ______________________________________

Publication Date: ____________________________________

Internal Links (Within Site):

____

____

External Links (Out of Site):

____

____

Click to Tweet: ______ Content Upgrade: ______

Images:

____

____

Post 4 Title: ____

Main Points:

____

____

____

____

____

____

Call to Action: ______________________________________

Publication Date: ____________________________________

Internal Links (Within Site):

____

____

External Links (Out of Site):

____

____

Click to Tweet: ________ Content Upgrade: ________

Images:

____

____

Post 5 Title: ______________________________

Main Points:

____

____

____

____

____

____

Call to Action: ______________________________

Publication Date: ______________________________

Internal Links (Within Site):

____

____

External Links (Out of Site):

____

____

Click to Tweet: ________ Content Upgrade: ________

Images:

____

____

Monthly Content Overview

Month: ____________________________

Theme: ____________________________

Goal: ____________________________

Post 1 Title/Topic: ____________________________

Post 2 Title/Topic: ____________________________

Post 3 Title/Topic: ____________________________

Post 4 Title/Topic: ____________________________

Post 5 Title/Topic: ____________________________

Post 6 Title/Topic: ____________________________

Special This Month

Events/Holidays:

Any special promotions (product/service):

Monthly Metrics

		Post 1	Post 2	Post 3	Post 4	Post 5	Post 6	Other
# of Page Visits								
# New Subscribers (Added to List)								
# of Sales (if applicable)								
New Followers: Facebook								
New Followers: LinkedIn								
New Followers: Twitter								
New Followers: Pinterest								
New Followers: Instagram								
New Followers:								
New Followers:								
# of Comments on Blog								

Share Tracker

	Post 1	Post 2	Post 3	Post 4	Post 5	Post 6	Other	Special
Email/Subscriber List								
Facebook Personal Page								
Facebook Fan/Biz Page								
LinkedIn								
Twitter								
Instagram								
Pinterest								
Other Social Media								
Other Social Media								
Group or Forum								
Group or Forum								
YouTube								
Other								
Other								
Other								

Post 1 Title: ______________________________

Main Points:

____

____

____

____

____

____

Call to Action: ______________________________

Publication Date: ______________________________

Internal Links (Within Site):

____

____

External Links (Out of Site):

____

____

Click to Tweet: ________ Content Upgrade: ________

Images:

____

____

Post 2 Title: ______________________________

Main Points:

____

____

____

____

____

____

Call to Action: ______________________________

Publication Date: ______________________________

Internal Links (Within Site):

____

____

External Links (Out of Site):

____

____

Click to Tweet: ________ Content Upgrade: ________

Images:

____

____

Post 3 Title: ____

Main Points:

____

____

____

____

____

____

Call to Action: ____________________________________

Publication Date: ____________________________________

Internal Links (Within Site):

____

____

External Links (Out of Site):

____

____

Click to Tweet: ________ Content Upgrade: ________

Images:

____

____

Post 4 Title: ______________________________

Main Points:

____

____

____

____

____

____

Call to Action: ______________________________

Publication Date: ______________________________

Internal Links (Within Site):

____

____

External Links (Out of Site):

____

____

Click to Tweet: ________ Content Upgrade: ________

Images:

____

____

Post 5 Title: ______________________________

Main Points:

____

____

____

____

____

____

Call to Action: ______________________________

Publication Date: ______________________________

Internal Links (Within Site):

____

____

External Links (Out of Site):

____

____

Click to Tweet: ________ Content Upgrade: ________

Images:

____

____

Monthly Content Overview

Month: ______________________________

Theme: ______________________________

Goal: ______________________________

Post 1 Title/Topic: ______________________________

Post 2 Title/Topic: ______________________________

Post 3 Title/Topic: ______________________________

Post 4 Title/Topic: ______________________________

Post 5 Title/Topic: ______________________________

Post 6 Title/Topic: ______________________________

Special This Month

Events/Holidays:

Any special promotions (product/service):

Monthly Metrics

		Post 1	Post 2	Post 3	Post 4	Post 5	Post 6	Other
# of Page Visits								
# New Subscribers (Added to List)								
# of Sales (if applicable)								
New Followers: Facebook								
New Followers: LinkedIn								
New Followers: Twitter								
New Followers: Pinterest								
New Followers: Instagram								
New Followers:								
New Followers:								
# of Comments on Blog								

Share Tracker

	Post 1	Post 2	Post 3	Post 4	Post 5	Post 6	Other	Special
Email/Subscriber List								
Facebook Personal Page								
Facebook Fan/Biz Page								
LinkedIn								
Twitter								
Instagram								
Pinterest								
Other Social Media								
Other Social Media								
Group or Forum								
Group or Forum								
YouTube								
Other								
Other								
Other								

Post 1 Title: ____

Main Points:

____

____

____

____

____

____

Call to Action: ______________________________________

Publication Date: ____________________________________

Internal Links (Within Site):

____

____

External Links (Out of Site):

____

____

Click to Tweet: ________ Content Upgrade: ________

Images:

____

____

Post 2 Title: ______________________________

Main Points:

____

____

____

____

____

____

Call to Action: ______________________________

Publication Date: ______________________________

Internal Links (Within Site):

____

____

External Links (Out of Site):

____

____

Click to Tweet: ________ Content Upgrade: ________

Images:

____

____

Post 3 Title: ______________________________

Main Points:

____

____

____

____

____

____

Call to Action: ______________________________

Publication Date: ______________________________

Internal Links (Within Site):

____

____

External Links (Out of Site):

____

____

Click to Tweet: ________ Content Upgrade: ________

Images:

____

____

Post 4 Title: ____

Main Points:

____

____

____

____

____

____

Call to Action: ______________________________________

Publication Date: ____________________________________

Internal Links (Within Site):

____

____

External Links (Out of Site):

____

____

Click to Tweet: ________ Content Upgrade: ________

Images:

____

____

Post 5 Title: ____

Main Points:

____

____

____

____

____

____

Call to Action: ______________________________________

Publication Date: ____________________________________

Internal Links (Within Site):

____

____

External Links (Out of Site):

____

____

Click to Tweet: ________ Content Upgrade: ________

Images:

____

____

Monthly Content Overview

Month: ______________________________

Theme: ______________________________

Goal: ______________________________

Post 1 Title/Topic: ______________________________

Post 2 Title/Topic: ______________________________

Post 3 Title/Topic: ______________________________

Post 4 Title/Topic: ______________________________

Post 5 Title/Topic: ______________________________

Post 6 Title/Topic: ______________________________

Special This Month

Events/Holidays:

Any special promotions (product/service):

Monthly Metrics

		Post 1	Post 2	Post 3	Post 4	Post 5	Post 6	Other
# of Page Visits								
# New Subscribers (Added to List)								
# of Sales (if applicable)								
New Followers: Facebook								
New Followers: LinkedIn								
New Followers: Twitter								
New Followers: Pinterest								
New Followers: Instagram								
New Followers:								
New Followers:								
# of Comments on Blog								

Share Tracker

	Post 1	Post 2	Post 3	Post 4	Post 5	Post 6	Other	Special
Email/Subscriber List								
Facebook Personal Page								
Facebook Fan/Biz Page								
LinkedIn								
Twitter								
Instagram								
Pinterest								
Other Social Media								
Other Social Media								
Group or Forum								
Group or Forum								
YouTube								
Other								
Other								
Other								

Post 1 Title: ____

Main Points:

____

____

____

____

____

____

Call to Action: ______________________________________

Publication Date: ____________________________________

Internal Links (Within Site):

____

____

External Links (Out of Site):

____

____

Click to Tweet: ________ Content Upgrade: ________

Images:

____

____

Post 2 Title: ____

Main Points:

____

____

____

____

____

____

Call to Action: ______________________________________

Publication Date: ____________________________________

Internal Links (Within Site):

____

____

External Links (Out of Site):

____

____

Click to Tweet: ______ Content Upgrade: ______

Images:

____

____

Post 3 Title: ____

Main Points:

____

____

____

____

____

____

Call to Action: ____________________________________

Publication Date: __________________________________

Internal Links (Within Site):

____

____

External Links (Out of Site):

____

____

Click to Tweet: ________ Content Upgrade: ________

Images:

____

____

Post 4 Title: ______________________________

Main Points:

____

____

____

____

____

____

Call to Action: ______________________________

Publication Date: ______________________________

Internal Links (Within Site):

____

____

External Links (Out of Site):

____

____

Click to Tweet: ________ Content Upgrade: ________

Images:

____

____

Post 5 Title: ____

Main Points:

____

____

____

____

____

____

Call to Action: ______________________________________

Publication Date: ____________________________________

Internal Links (Within Site):

____

____

External Links (Out of Site):

____

____

Click to Tweet: ______ Content Upgrade: ______

Images:

____

____

Monthly Content Overview

Month: ______________________________

Theme: ______________________________

Goal: ______________________________

Post 1 Title/Topic: ______________________________

Post 2 Title/Topic: ______________________________

Post 3 Title/Topic: ______________________________

Post 4 Title/Topic: ______________________________

Post 5 Title/Topic: ______________________________

Post 6 Title/Topic: ______________________________

Special This Month

Events/Holidays:

Any special promotions (product/service):

Monthly Metrics

		Post 1	Post 2	Post 3	Post 4	Post 5	Post 6	Other
# of Page Visits								
# New Subscribers (Added to List)								
# of Sales (if applicable)								
New Followers: Facebook								
New Followers: LinkedIn								
New Followers: Twitter								
New Followers: Pinterest								
New Followers: Instagram								
New Followers:								
New Followers:								
# of Comments on Blog								

Share Tracker

	Post 1	Post 2	Post 3	Post 4	Post 5	Post 6	Other	Special
Email/Subscriber List								
Facebook Personal Page								
Facebook Fan/Biz Page								
LinkedIn								
Twitter								
Instagram								
Pinterest								
Other Social Media								
Other Social Media								
Group or Forum								
Group or Forum								
YouTube								
Other								
Other								
Other								

Post 1 Title: ____

Main Points:

____

____

____

____

____

____

Call to Action: ______________________________________

Publication Date: ____________________________________

Internal Links (Within Site):

____

____

External Links (Out of Site):

____

____

Click to Tweet: ________ Content Upgrade: ________

Images:

____

____

Post 2 Title: ____

Main Points:

____

____

____

____

____

____

Call to Action: ______________________________________

Publication Date: ____________________________________

Internal Links (Within Site):

____

____

External Links (Out of Site):

____

____

Click to Tweet: ________ Content Upgrade: ________

Images:

____

____

Post 3 Title: ______________________________

Main Points:

____

____

____

____

____

____

Call to Action: ______________________________

Publication Date: ______________________________

Internal Links (Within Site):

____

____

External Links (Out of Site):

____

____

Click to Tweet: ________ Content Upgrade: ________

Images:

____

____

Post 4 Title: ______________________________

Main Points:

____

____

____

____

____

____

Call to Action: ______________________________

Publication Date: ______________________________

Internal Links (Within Site):

____

____

External Links (Out of Site):

____

____

Click to Tweet: ________ Content Upgrade: ________

Images:

____

____

Post 5 Title: ____________________

Main Points:

____

____

____

____

____

____

Call to Action: ____________________

Publication Date: ____________________

Internal Links (Within Site):

____

____

External Links (Out of Site):

____

____

Click to Tweet: ________ Content Upgrade: ________

Images:

____

____

Monthly Content Overview

Month: ______________________________

Theme: ______________________________

Goal: ______________________________

Post 1 Title/Topic: ______________________________

Post 2 Title/Topic: ______________________________

Post 3 Title/Topic: ______________________________

Post 4 Title/Topic: ______________________________

Post 5 Title/Topic: ______________________________

Post 6 Title/Topic: ______________________________

Special This Month

Events/Holidays:

Any special promotions (product/service):

Monthly Metrics

		Post 1	Post 2	Post 3	Post 4	Post 5	Post 6	Other
# of Page Visits								
# New Subscribers (Added to List)								
# of Sales (if applicable)								
New Followers: Facebook								
New Followers: LinkedIn								
New Followers: Twitter								
New Followers: Pinterest								
New Followers: Instagram								
New Followers:								
New Followers:								
# of Comments on Blog								

Share Tracker

	Post 1	Post 2	Post 3	Post 4	Post 5	Post 6	Other	Special
Email/Subscriber List								
Facebook Personal Page								
Facebook Fan/Biz Page								
LinkedIn								
Twitter								
Instagram								
Pinterest								
Other Social Media								
Other Social Media								
Group or Forum								
Group or Forum								
YouTube								
Other								
Other								
Other								

Post 1 Title: ____

Main Points:

____

____

____

____

____

____

Call to Action: ______________________________________

Publication Date: ____________________________________

Internal Links (Within Site):

____

____

External Links (Out of Site):

____

____

Click to Tweet: ______ Content Upgrade: ______

Images:

____

____

Post 2 Title: ______________________________

Main Points:

____

____

____

____

____

____

Call to Action: ______________________________

Publication Date: ______________________________

Internal Links (Within Site):

____

____

External Links (Out of Site):

____

____

Click to Tweet: ________ Content Upgrade: ________

Images:

____

____

Post 3 Title: ____

Main Points:

____

____

____

____

____

____

Call to Action: ______________________________________

Publication Date: ____________________________________

Internal Links (Within Site):

____

____

External Links (Out of Site):

____

____

Click to Tweet: ________ Content Upgrade: ________

Images:

____

____

Post 4 Title: ____

Main Points:

____

____

____

____

____

____

Call to Action: ______________________________________

Publication Date: ____________________________________

Internal Links (Within Site):

____

____

External Links (Out of Site):

____

____

Click to Tweet: ________ Content Upgrade: ________

Images:

____

____

Post 5 Title: ______________________________

Main Points:

____

____

____

____

____

____

Call to Action: ______________________________

Publication Date: ______________________________

Internal Links (Within Site):

____

____

External Links (Out of Site):

____

____

Click to Tweet: ________ Content Upgrade: ________

Images:

____

____

Monthly Content Overview

Month: ______________________________

Theme: ______________________________

Goal: ______________________________

Post 1 Title/Topic: ______________________________

Post 2 Title/Topic: ______________________________

Post 3 Title/Topic: ______________________________

Post 4 Title/Topic: ______________________________

Post 5 Title/Topic: ______________________________

Post 6 Title/Topic: ______________________________

Special This Month

Events/Holidays:

Any special promotions (product/service):

Monthly Metrics

		Post 1	Post 2	Post 3	Post 4	Post 5	Post 6	Other
# of Page Visits								
# New Subscribers (Added to List)								
# of Sales (if applicable)								
New Followers: Facebook								
New Followers: LinkedIn								
New Followers: Twitter								
New Followers: Pinterest								
New Followers: Instagram								
New Followers:								
New Followers:								
# of Comments on Blog								

Share Tracker

	Post 1	Post 2	Post 3	Post 4	Post 5	Post 6	Other	Special
Email/Subscriber List								
Facebook Personal Page								
Facebook Fan/Biz Page								
LinkedIn								
Twitter								
Instagram								
Pinterest								
Other Social Media								
Other Social Media								
Group or Forum								
Group or Forum								
YouTube								
Other								
Other								
Other								

Post 1 Title: ____

Main Points:

____

____

____

____

____

____

Call to Action: ____________________________________

Publication Date: ____________________________________

Internal Links (Within Site):

____

____

External Links (Out of Site):

____

____

Click to Tweet: ________ Content Upgrade: ________

Images:

____

____

Post 2 Title: ____

Main Points:

____

____

____

____

____

____

Call to Action: ______________________________________

Publication Date: ____________________________________

Internal Links (Within Site):

____

____

External Links (Out of Site):

____

____

Click to Tweet: ________ Content Upgrade: ________

Images:

____

____

Post 3 Title: ______________________________

Main Points:

____

____

____

____

____

____

Call to Action: ______________________________

Publication Date: ______________________________

Internal Links (Within Site):

____

____

External Links (Out of Site):

____

____

Click to Tweet: ________ Content Upgrade: ________

Images:

____

____

Post 4 Title: ____

Main Points:

____

____

____

____

____

____

Call to Action: ____

Publication Date: ____

Internal Links (Within Site):

____

____

External Links (Out of Site):

____

____

Click to Tweet: ________

Content Upgrade: ________

Images:

____

____

Post 5 Title: ______________________________

Main Points:

____

____

____

____

____

____

Call to Action: ______________________________

Publication Date: ______________________________

Internal Links (Within Site):

____

____

External Links (Out of Site):

____

____

Click to Tweet: ________ Content Upgrade: ________

Images:

____

____

Monthly Content Overview

Month: ______________________________

Theme: ______________________________

Goal: ______________________________

Post 1 Title/Topic: ______________________________

Post 2 Title/Topic: ______________________________

Post 3 Title/Topic: ______________________________

Post 4 Title/Topic: ______________________________

Post 5 Title/Topic: ______________________________

Post 6 Title/Topic: ______________________________

Special This Month

Events/Holidays:

Any special promotions (product/service):

Monthly Metrics

		Post 1	Post 2	Post 3	Post 4	Post 5	Post 6	Other
# of Page Visits								
# New Subscribers (Added to List)								
# of Sales (if applicable)								
New Followers: Facebook								
New Followers: LinkedIn								
New Followers: Twitter								
New Followers: Pinterest								
New Followers: Instagram								
New Followers:								
New Followers:								
# of Comments on Blog								

Share Tracker

	Post 1	Post 2	Post 3	Post 4	Post 5	Post 6	Other	Special
Email/Subscriber List								
Facebook Personal Page								
Facebook Fan/Biz Page								
LinkedIn								
Twitter								
Instagram								
Pinterest								
Other Social Media								
Other Social Media								
Group or Forum								
Group or Forum								
YouTube								
Other								
Other								
Other								

Post 1 Title: ____

Main Points:

____

____

____

____

____

____

Call to Action: ____________________________________

Publication Date: __________________________________

Internal Links (Within Site):

____

____

External Links (Out of Site):

____

____

Click to Tweet: ______ Content Upgrade: ______

Images:

____

____

Post 2 Title: ______________________________

Main Points:

____

____

____

____

____

____

Call to Action: ______________________________

Publication Date: ______________________________

Internal Links (Within Site):

____

____

External Links (Out of Site):

____

____

Click to Tweet: ________ Content Upgrade: ________

Images:

____

____

Post 3 Title: ______________________________

Main Points:

____

____

____

____

____

____

Call to Action: ______________________________

Publication Date: ______________________________

Internal Links (Within Site):

____

____

External Links (Out of Site):

____

____

Click to Tweet: ________ Content Upgrade: ________

Images:

____

____

Post 4 Title: ______________________________

Main Points:

____

____

____

____

____

____

Call to Action: ______________________________

Publication Date: ______________________________

Internal Links (Within Site):

____

____

External Links (Out of Site):

____

____

Click to Tweet: ________ Content Upgrade: ________

Images:

____

____

Post 5 Title: ______________________________

Main Points:

____

____

____

____

____

____

Call to Action: ______________________________

Publication Date: ______________________________

Internal Links (Within Site):

____

____

External Links (Out of Site):

____

____

Click to Tweet: ________ Content Upgrade: ________

Images:

____

____

Monthly Content Overview

Month: ____________________________________

Theme: ____________________________________

Goal: ____________________________________

Post 1 Title/Topic: ____________________________________

Post 2 Title/Topic: ____________________________________

Post 3 Title/Topic: ____________________________________

Post 4 Title/Topic: ____________________________________

Post 5 Title/Topic: ____________________________________

Post 6 Title/Topic: ____________________________________

Special This Month

Events/Holidays:

Any special promotions (product/service):

Monthly Metrics

		Post 1	Post 2	Post 3	Post 4	Post 5	Post 6	Other
# of Page Visits								
# New Subscribers (Added to List)								
# of Sales (if applicable)								
New Followers: Facebook								
New Followers: LinkedIn								
New Followers: Twitter								
New Followers: Pinterest								
New Followers: Instagram								
New Followers:								
New Followers:								
# of Comments on Blog								

Share Tracker

	Post 1	Post 2	Post 3	Post 4	Post 5	Post 6	Other	Special
Email/Subscriber List								
Facebook Personal Page								
Facebook Fan/Biz Page								
LinkedIn								
Twitter								
Instagram								
Pinterest								
Other Social Media								
Other Social Media								
Group or Forum								
Group or Forum								
YouTube								
Other								
Other								
Other								

Post 1 Title: ______________________________

Main Points:

____

____

____

____

____

____

Call to Action: ______________________________

Publication Date: ______________________________

Internal Links (Within Site):

____

____

External Links (Out of Site):

____

____

Click to Tweet: ________ Content Upgrade: ________

Images:

____

____

Post 2 Title: ____

Main Points:

____

____

____

____

____

____

Call to Action: ______________________________________

Publication Date: ____________________________________

Internal Links (Within Site):

____

____

External Links (Out of Site):

____

____

Click to Tweet: ________ Content Upgrade: ________

Images:

____

____

Post 3 Title: ____

Main Points:

____

____

____

____

____

____

Call to Action: ______________________________________

Publication Date: ____________________________________

Internal Links (Within Site):

____

____

External Links (Out of Site):

____

____

Click to Tweet: ________ Content Upgrade: ________

Images:

____

____

Post 4 Title: ____

Main Points:

____

____

____

____

____

____

Call to Action: ______________________________________

Publication Date: ____________________________________

Internal Links (Within Site):

____

____

External Links (Out of Site):

____

____

Click to Tweet: ________ Content Upgrade: ________

Images:

____

____

Post 5 Title: ______________________________

Main Points:

____

____

____

____

____

____

Call to Action: ______________________________

Publication Date: ______________________________

Internal Links (Within Site):

____

____

External Links (Out of Site):

____

____

Click to Tweet: ________ Content Upgrade: ________

Images:

____

____

Monthly Content Overview

Month: ______________________________

Theme: ______________________________

Goal: ______________________________

Post 1 Title/Topic: ______________________________

Post 2 Title/Topic: ______________________________

Post 3 Title/Topic: ______________________________

Post 4 Title/Topic: ______________________________

Post 5 Title/Topic: ______________________________

Post 6 Title/Topic: ______________________________

Special This Month

Events/Holidays:

Any special promotions (product/service):

Monthly Metrics

		Post 1	Post 2	Post 3	Post 4	Post 5	Post 6	Other
# of Page Visits								
# New Subscribers (Added to List)								
# of Sales (if applicable)								
New Followers: Facebook								
New Followers: LinkedIn								
New Followers: Twitter								
New Followers: Pinterest								
New Followers: Instagram								
New Followers:								
New Followers:								
# of Comments on Blog								

Share Tracker

	Post 1	Post 2	Post 3	Post 4	Post 5	Post 6	Other	Special
Email/Subscriber List								
Facebook Personal Page								
Facebook Fan/Biz Page								
LinkedIn								
Twitter								
Instagram								
Pinterest								
Other Social Media								
Other Social Media								
Group or Forum								
Group or Forum								
YouTube								
Other								
Other								
Other								

Post 1 Title: ______________________________

Main Points:

____

____

____

____

____

____

Call to Action: ______________________________

Publication Date: ______________________________

Internal Links (Within Site):

____

____

External Links (Out of Site):

____

____

Click to Tweet: ________ Content Upgrade: ________

Images:

____

____

Post 2 Title: ____

Main Points:

____

____

____

____

____

____

Call to Action: ______________________________________

Publication Date: ____________________________________

Internal Links (Within Site):

____

____

External Links (Out of Site):

____

____

Click to Tweet: ________ Content Upgrade: ________

Images:

____

____

Post 3 Title: ____

Main Points:

____

____

____

____

____

____

Call to Action: ______________________________________

Publication Date: ____________________________________

Internal Links (Within Site):

____

____

External Links (Out of Site):

____

____

Click to Tweet: ________ Content Upgrade: ________

Images:

____

____

Post 4 Title: ______________________________

Main Points:

____

____

____

____

____

____

Call to Action: ______________________________

Publication Date: ______________________________

Internal Links (Within Site):

____

____

External Links (Out of Site):

____

____

Click to Tweet: ________ Content Upgrade: ________

Images:

____

____

Post 5 Title: ____________________

Main Points:

____

____

____

____

____

____

Call to Action: ____________________

Publication Date: ____________________

Internal Links (Within Site):

____

____

External Links (Out of Site):

____

____

Click to Tweet: ________ Content Upgrade: ________

Images:

____

____

Monthly Content Overview

Month: ____

Theme: ____

Goal: ____

Post 1 Title/Topic: ____

Post 2 Title/Topic: ____

Post 3 Title/Topic: ____

Post 4 Title/Topic: ____

Post 5 Title/Topic: ____

Post 6 Title/Topic: ____

Special This Month

Events/Holidays:

Any special promotions (product/service):

Monthly Metrics

		Post 1	Post 2	Post 3	Post 4	Post 5	Post 6	Other
# of Page Visits								
# New Subscribers (Added to List)								
# of Sales (if applicable)								
New Followers: Facebook								
New Followers: LinkedIn								
New Followers: Twitter								
New Followers: Pinterest								
New Followers: Instagram								
New Followers:								
New Followers:								
# of Comments on Blog								

Share Tracker

	Post 1	Post 2	Post 3	Post 4	Post 5	Post 6	Other	Special
Email/Subscriber List								
Facebook Personal Page								
Facebook Fan/Biz Page								
LinkedIn								
Twitter								
Instagram								
Pinterest								
Other Social Media								
Other Social Media								
Group or Forum								
Group or Forum								
YouTube								
Other								
Other								
Other								

Post 1 Title: ____

Main Points:

____

____

____

____

____

____

Call to Action: ______________________________________

Publication Date: ____________________________________

Internal Links (Within Site):

____

____

External Links (Out of Site):

____

____

Click to Tweet: ________ Content Upgrade: ________

Images:

____

____

Post 2 Title: ____

Main Points:

____

____

____

____

____

____

Call to Action: ______________________________________

Publication Date: ____________________________________

Internal Links (Within Site):

____

____

External Links (Out of Site):

____

____

Click to Tweet: ________ Content Upgrade: ________

Images:

____

____

Post 3 Title: ____________________

Main Points:

____

____

____

____

____

____

Call to Action: ____________________

Publication Date: ____________________

Internal Links (Within Site):

____

____

External Links (Out of Site):

____

____

Click to Tweet: ________ Content Upgrade: ________

Images:

____

____

Post 4 Title: ____________________

Main Points:

____

____

____

____

____

____

Call to Action: ____________________

Publication Date: ____________________

Internal Links (Within Site):

____

____

External Links (Out of Site):

____

____

Click to Tweet: ________ Content Upgrade: ________

Images:

____

____

Post 5 Title: ____________________

Main Points:

____

____

____

____

____

____

Call to Action: ____________________

Publication Date: ____________________

Internal Links (Within Site):

____

____

External Links (Out of Site):

____

____

Click to Tweet: ________ Content Upgrade: ________

Images:

____

____

Made in the USA
Las Vegas, NV
03 November 2026

57424667R00069